Baby Animals Grow

Jill Malcolm

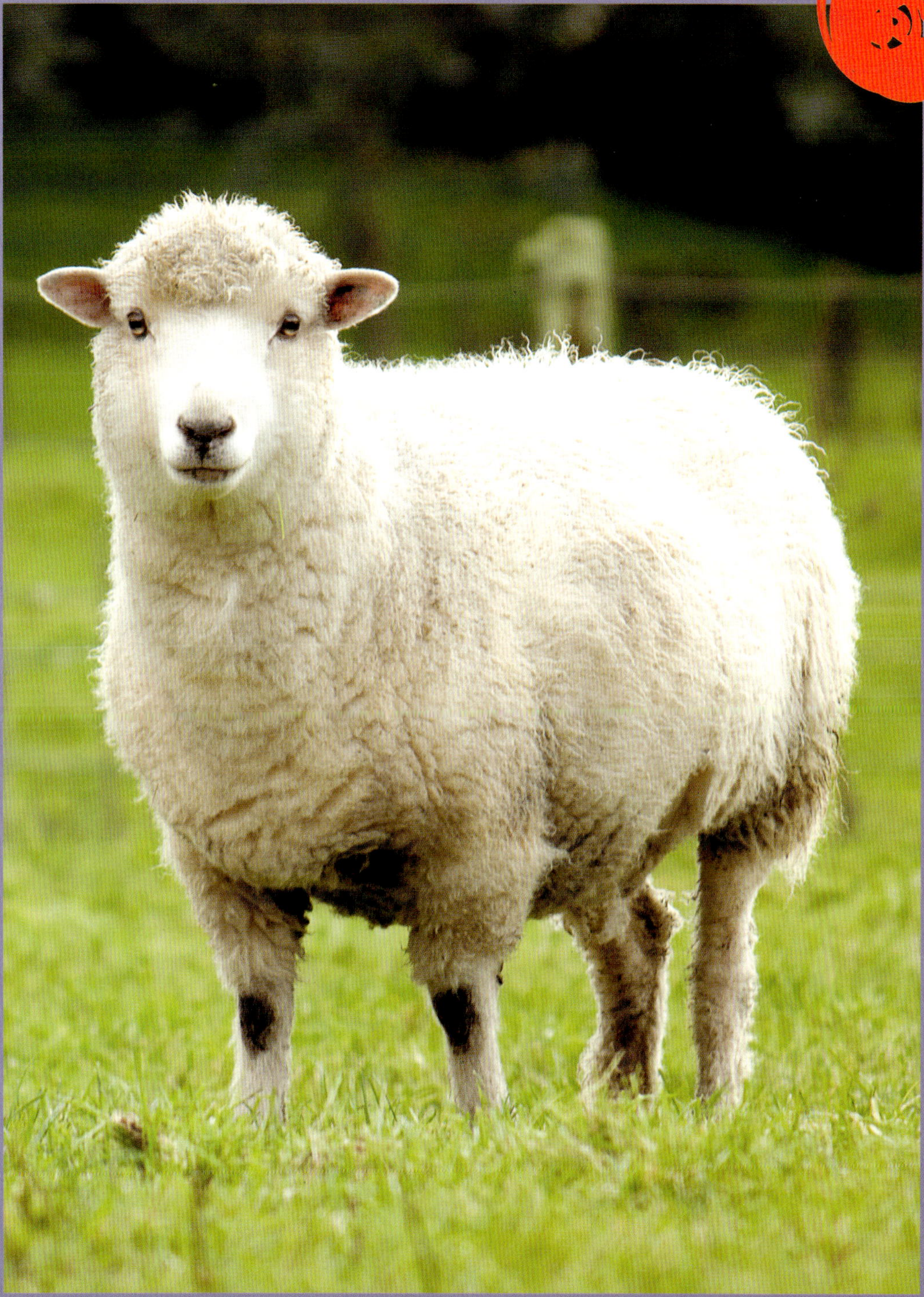

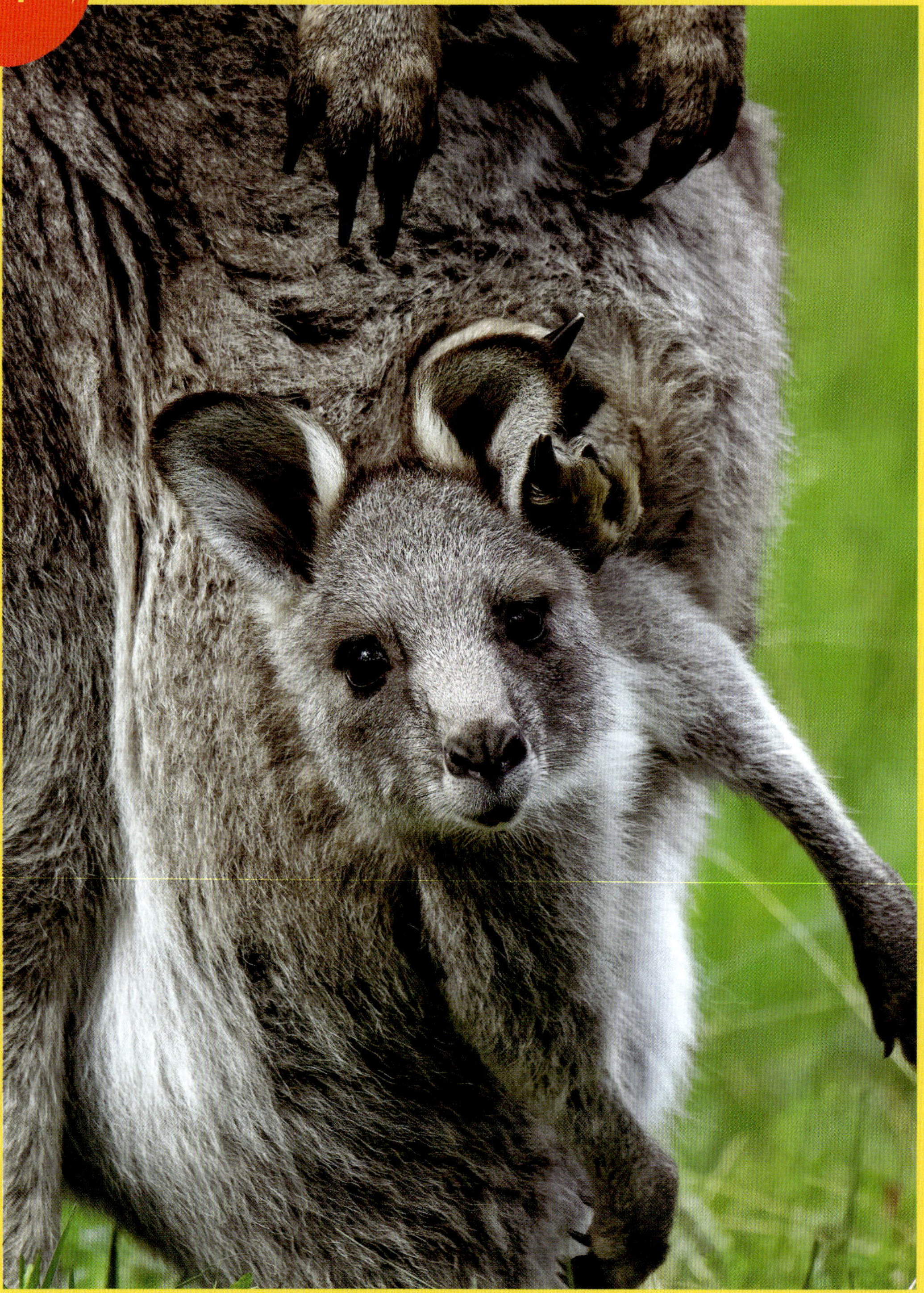

Notes for the Grown-ups

This wordless book allows for a rich shared reading experience for children who do not yet know how to read words or who are beginning to learn. Children can look at the pages to gather information from what they see, and they can suggest text to tell the story.

To extend this reading experience, do one or more of the following:

Have fun making the sounds animals make. Do the babies make different sounds than the grown animals do?

Introduce vocabulary such as these words when looking at the pictures and telling the story you see:

- cub, tiger
- duckling, duck
- fawn, deer
- joey, kangaroo
- kitten, cat

- lamb, sheep
- piglet, pig
- pup, shark
- puppy, dog
- tadpole, frog

There are many baby and grown animals in this book. Can the child name them all? How do the baby and adult animals differ?

After reading the pictures, come back to the book again and again. Rereading is an excellent tool for building literacy skills.

Talk about things that human babies have in common with animal babies and also all the things that are different.

Consultant

Cynthia Malo, M.A.Ed.

Publishing Credits

Rachelle Cracchiolo, M.S.Ed., *Publisher*
Emily R. Smith, M.A.Ed., *SVP of Content Development*
Véronique Bos, *VP of Creative*
Dona Herweck Rice, *Senior Content Manager*

Image Credits: all images from iStock and/or Shutterstock

Library of Congress Cataloging in Publication Control Number:
2024013682

5482 Argosy Avenue
Huntington Beach, CA 92649
www.tcmpub.com
ISBN 979-8-7659-6145-2
© 2025 Teacher Created Materials, Inc.
Printed by: 926. Printed In: Malaysia. PO#: PO11723